30-Second CNN World News:
Culture and Society
in a Changing World

Yasushi Mano

Asahi Press

音声再生アプリ「リスニング・トレーナー」を使った音声ダウンロード

朝日出版社開発のアプリ、「リスニング・トレーナー（リストレ）」を使えば、教科書の音声をスマホ、タブレットに簡単にダウンロードできます。どうぞご活用ください。

◉ アプリ【リスニング・トレーナー】の使い方

《アプリのダウンロード》

App Store または Google Play から「リスニング・トレーナー」のアプリ（無料）をダウンロード

App Store はこちら▶

Google Play はこちら▶

《アプリの使い方》

① アプリを開き「コンテンツを追加」をタップ
② 画面上部に【15669】を入力しDoneをタップ

音声ストリーミング配信 》》》

この教科書の音声は、右記ウェブサイトにて無料で配信しています。

https://text.asahipress.com/free/english/

はしがき

　語学はスポーツや楽器と同様、上達するのに時間がかかります。学校の授業や教科書の役割は、みなさんに学習上のヒントを差し上げること、またそれと同じくらい大事なのが、ことばに対するみなさんの興味関心を刺激して高めること。そんな考え方で、この本は編まれています。

　素材には、月刊英語学習誌『CNN English Express』の短いニュース記事と音声から、話題となる国や地域はもちろん、アンカーパーソンの英語も多様になるように選びました。音声は、実際のCNNの放送で流れた「ナチュラル」のほかに、ナレーターが読み直した「ゆっくり（ポーズなし）」と「ゆっくり（ポーズあり）」も用意しました。目的に応じて3種類の音声をお使いください。なお、「ナチュラル」のスピードですと、各ユニット35秒前後です。

　各ユニットの構成を簡単に説明しておきます。

　リスニングの前に、各ユニットの内容と間接的にかかわるクイズのような"Choose the suitable words to fill in the blanks."があります。なかには難しいものもありますから、わからなくても、間違っても、がっかりしないでください。インターネットなどを使って調べ物をする練習のつもりで取り組んでいただければ結構です。

　次の"Key Words"では、英語のことばの英語による定義に慣れていただければと思います。英和辞典だけでなく英英辞典も使うようになるきっかけとなることを願っています。

　さて、リスニングです。自信のある方は、一度はテキストを見ないで聴いてください。自信がなければ、最初は文字を見ながら聴き、二度目、三度目に文字を見ずに聴くのもよいでしょう。リスニングのテキストには埋めるべき穴を三つ設けました。聴き取るのが容易でないことを承知の上で、数字や固有名詞が出てくるところを多く空所にしてあります。

　リスニングのあとは、"True or False?"と"Choose the correct answer."に答えることによって、内容が理解できたかを、また、Notesによって語彙を、それぞれ確認してください。語彙力に不安のある場合は、リスニングの前に語彙に目を通しておく手もあります。

　「ここ、よく聴いてみて」はリスニングのヒントです。ポイントは二つ。まず、実際の英語は一つ一つの音を区切って言うわけではありませんから、音のつながり具合に注意してもらうこと。もう一つは、アメリカ英語とはちょっと違うイギリス英語やオーストラリア英語にも馴染んでもらうこと。

　しめくくりの「イディオムをもう1つ」は、各ユニットに出てきた表現に直接、間接に関係する慣用句をもう1つ覚えようという、ちょっと欲張ったコーナーです。英語には非常に多くのイディオムがあり、それが英語を奥の深い、つまり面白くて難しい、難しいけれど面白い言語にしていますから、ぜひ、関心をもっていただきたいと思いました。

　本書はリスニングに主眼を置いた副教材として構想されました。ですが、使い方は使う方次第。なんらかの形でみなさんのお役に立つことができれば嬉しく存じます。ご質問ご意見などございましたら、ご遠慮なく編集部までお寄せください。

　この企画は、ずいぶん昔からの知り合いである編集部の小川洋一郎さんが持ってきてくださって、実際の編集では今回はじめて知り合った加藤愛理さんがお世話くださり、おかげさまで楽しく書くことができました。また、英文は、田所メアリーさんが丁寧に見てくださいました。この場をお借りして、お三方に厚くお礼申し上げます。

2020年冬　真野　泰

Contents >>>

30-Second CNN World News:
Culture and Society
in a Changing World

Unit 1

Void Found in Giza's Great Pyramid

クフ王ピラミッドの内部に不思議な巨大空間

わたしたちはなぜ、ピラミッドをピラミッドと呼ぶのでしょう？ピラミッドの語源 (etymology) をたどっていくと……結局よくわからない。それに、実物の構造もまだまだ謎だらけのようです。

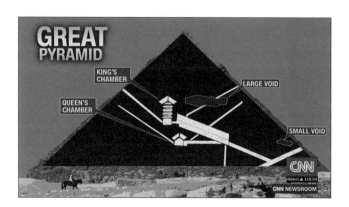

 **Before listening**

✣ Choose the suitable words to fill in the blanks.

Giza is a city in (**1**   ), located on the western bank of the (**2**   ) River. Rising just west of the city are the Great (**3**   ) and the Pyramids of Giza, which are believed to have been built in the 26th century BC.

- (**1**)   **a.** Egypt   **b.** Greece   **c.** Mongolia   **d.** Saudi Arabia
- (**2**)   **a.** Amazon   **b.** Congo   **c.** Mekong   **d.** Nile
- (**3**)   **a.** Dragon   **b.** Griffin   **c.** Phoenix   **d.** Sphinx

Key Words

Which one of the following words best suits each definition?

> ancient / cavity / chamber / cosmic / void

(1　　　) : a hole inside something solid

(2　　　) : a large empty space

(3　　　) : a room used for a special purpose

(4　　　) : belonging to a time long ago in history

(5　　　) : relating to outer space or the universe

02
ナチュラル

03
ゆっくり
〈ポーズなし〉

04
ゆっくり
〈ポーズあり〉

 Listening

アメリカ英語

❖ Listen carefully and fill in the blanks.

We want to share with you now a new discovery about an ancient monument.// Scientists are scratching their (**1**　　　) about a mysterious void/ in the heart of the Great Pyramid at Giza in Egypt.// They're not allowed to drill into the structure,/ so they use technology that employs cosmic rays to visualize the interior.// The void is as big as a passenger plane/ and was unknown for (**2**　　　) years.// It's one of four cavities in the pyramid,/ along with the King's and Queen's Chambers and the Grand Gallery,/ but it has no (**3**　　　).//

(November 3, 2017)

 **After listening**

<< **True** <or> **False?** >>

(1) Scientists now fully understand why there is a large void in the heart of the Great Pyramid.

(2) Apart from the newly discovered void, there are three cavities in the Great Pyramid.

❖ Choose the correct answer.

(1) What method did the scientists use to see the inside of the Great Pyramid?

    a. A high-speed, electric drill.

    b. Technology that employs ultrasonic waves.

    c. Technology that makes use of radiation from space.

              (   )

(2) How large is the newly found void?

    a. It is as big as a human heart.

    b. It is the size of an airliner.

    c. Its size is still under investigation.

              (   )

Notes

void ● 空間、虚空、空洞

the Great Pyramid (of Giza) ● ギザの大ピラミッド
（3つある大ピラミッドのうち、特にクフ王のもの）

ancient ● 古代の

monument ● 記念建造物、モニュメント

scratch one's head ● 頭をかく、（答えがわからなくて）首をひねる

in the heart of ... ● 〜の中心部に

be allowed to do ● 〜することが許されている

drill into ... ● 〜に穴をあける

structure ● 構造；構築物、建造物

employ ● （人を）使用する、雇用する；（手段を）使用する、用いる

cosmic ray ● 宇宙線

visualize ● 目に見えるようにする、視覚化する

interior ● 内部、内側

passenger plane ● 旅客機

cavity ● 固体の内部の空所、（体内の）腔、（虫歯の）穴

along with ... ● 〜と一緒に、〜に加えて、〜のほかに

chamber ● 部屋、室、（特に）寝室

the Grand Gallery ● （ギザの大ピラミッド内部の）大回廊

ここ、よく聴いてみて

　最終センテンスの出だしにある one of のあたりの音の連鎖に注意してみてください。はっきり2語に分けて「ワン・オヴ」とは発音されていませんね。「ワ（ン）ナフ」と、まるで1語のようにつながって、さらに次にくる four の f の音に続いていく。

　同じ文の最後の単語 entrance は聞き取りにくくありませんでしたか。「エントランス」とカタカナで書くと、まるで6つの音からできているように見えますが、英語は / én-trəns / と2音節。特に注意していただきたいのは、/ ntr / と子音が3つ連続するところと / ns / と子音が2つ連続するところ。こんなふうに聞こえるんですね。

イディオムをもう1つ

　日本語の「頭をかく」は照れ臭いときの仕草ですが、英語の scratch one's head（頭をかく）は答えを見つけようと一生懸命に考えているときの仕草です。

　ところで、頭をかくのは簡単ですが、背中は場所によって手が届きにくい。人にかいてもらいたくなることもありますね。英語には、"You scratch my back and I'll scratch yours."（背中をかいてよ、きみの背中をかいてあげるから）という決まり文句があります。どんな意味なのか、想像がつきますか？

2

Railway Apologizes for 20-Second Error

日本の鉄道会社、20秒早く発車して謝罪

形容詞 punctual（時間を厳守する）の語源にはラテン語の *punctum*（点）があります。つまり、punctual であるとは、ある時点（point of time）にピッタリということ。ですから、punctual は、neither early nor late と言い換えることができます。

JAPAN RAIL COMPANY SORRY TRAIN LEFT 20 SECONDS EARLY

 **Before listening**

♣ Choose the suitable words to fill in the blanks.

The world's first public railway opened in 1825 between Stockton and Darlington in Britain, using George Stephenson's (**1**　　) engine. By the middle of the (**2**　　)century the country was covered with railways. When the first railway in Japan opened in 1872 between Tokyo and (**3**　　), much of the equipment was provided by British manufacturers.

(1) **a.** diesel **b.** fire **c.** gasoline **d.** steam

(2) **a.** eighteen **b.** eighteenth **c.** nineteen **d.** nineteenth

(3) **a.** Hachiōji **b.** Odawara **c.** Utsunomiya **d.** Yokohama

Key Words

Which one of the following words best suits each definition?

> apology / commuter / departure / envious / premature

(1   ) : a word or statement saying sorry for doing something wrong

(2   ) : someone who regularly travels a long distance to work

(3   ) : the act of leaving a place

(4   ) : happening before the normal or proper time

(5   ) : wanting something that someone else has

ナチュラル　ゆっくり　ゆっくり
〈ポーズなし〉〈ポーズあり〉

🎧 Listening

オーストラリア英語

♣ Listen carefully and fill in the blanks.

Well, if a train goes off schedule,/ an apology can help soothe the frustration—/ make up (1   ) that terrible inconvenience you just suffered.// But media reports say/ a rail company in Japan took that (2   ) a whole new level/ by posting a formal apology when a train left the station 20 seconds early.// Now, Japan is known (3   ) politeness, precision, punctuality.// In this case,/ no one missed the train or even complained about the premature departure.// Commuters in many other countries are amused and envious.//

(November 17, 2017)

After listening

⟪ True ⟨or⟩ False? ⟫

(1) A Japanese railway company apologized after a train left the station only 20 seconds late.

(2) Japanese people are famous for being polite, precise, and punctual.

❖ Choose the correct answer.

(1) Why is it important to apologize when a train does not run on schedule?

    a. Because it helps make up for the lost time.

    b. Because it helps people feel less angry about what happened.

    c. Because it takes people's attention away from what happened.

(   )

(2) What happened when the train left the station 20 seconds early?

    a. No one missed the train and no complaint was made.

    b. No one missed the train, but someone made a complaint to the rail company.

    c. One person missed the train and made a complaint to the rail company.

(   )

Notes

railway ● 鉄道 (会社)	**politeness** ● 礼儀正しさ
apologize for ... ● 〜について謝罪する	**precision** ● 正確さ
go off schedule ● 予定からずれる	**punctuality** ● 時間厳守
apology ● 謝罪	**premature** ● 早すぎる、早まった
soothe ● (苦痛などを) 和らげる	**departure** ● 出発
make up for ... ● (損失などを) 埋め合わせる	**commuter** ● 通勤者
inconvenience ● 不都合、不便	**be amused** ● 面白がる
take ... to a whole new level	**envious** ● うらやんで
● 〜をまったくの別次元にまで引き上げる	

ここ、よく聴いてみて

　最初のセンテンスに出てくる schedule は聞き取れましたか？ オーストラリア英語の土台はイギリス英語。イギリスやオーストラリアでは、schedule は伝統的に / ʃɛdjuːl / (シェデュール) あるいは / ʃɛdʒjuːl / (シェヂュール) と発音されてきました。ただ、現在では、イギリスやオーストラリアでも、アメリカ流の / skɛdʒjuːl / (スケヂュール) という発音が増えつつあります。

　これは、もともと古いフランス語の *cedule* (今のフランス語の *cédule*) が14世紀末に英語に入り、英語でも最初は cedule あるいは sedule と綴られ、/ sɛdjuːl / (セデュール) と発音されていたからです。もとの意味は、「(文字の書かれた) 一片の紙」。

　ことばは時間のたつうちに綴りも、発音も、意味も変わっていくのですね。

イディオムをもう1つ

　イディオムというほどではありませんが、take someone to a place は「誰かをどこかへ連れていく」、take something to a place は「何かをどこかへ持っていく」の意。今回出てきた take that to a whole new level を直訳すると、「それ [列車運行に関して迷惑をかけたら謝ること] をまったく新しいレベルへ持っていく」とでもなるでしょうか。

　行儀の悪い子供を叱るときの伝統的な言い回しに、"I can't take you anywhere." があります。お前みたいな子は恥ずかしくてどこへも連れていけない、というわけです。もっと今回の表現に似た言い回しなら、take something to extremes(何かを極端へ持っていく)でしょうか。"Taken to extremes, some diets can be dangerous." (ダイエットによっては極端なやり方をすると危険なこともある)のように使います。

Observers Report Nine-Hour Rainbow

9時間も持続した虹

みなさんは虹の7色を順に言えますか？　英語では、Richard Of York Gave Battle In Vain.（ヨーク公リチャードは戦ったものの無益であった）と覚えるより。ほら、赤（red）、橙（orange）、黄（yellow）、緑（green）、青（blue）、藍（Indigo）、紫（violet）になっているでしょ。

TAIWAN RAINBOW LASTS "RECORD-BREAKING" NINE HOURS

Before listening

♣ Choose the suitable words to fill in the blanks.

According to Thai Buddhist legends, the rainbow is a (**1**   ) connecting heaven with earth down which the gods descend. This idea of the rainbow as a (**2**   ) between heaven and earth is also found in Greek mythology; Iris is the goddess of the rainbow and carries messages from the gods to (**3**   ).

(1)　**a.** corridor　**b.** garden　**c.** staircase　**d.** wall

(2)　**a.** barrier　**b.** bridge　**c.** gap　**d.** war

(3)　**a.** angels　**b.** heaven　**c.** humanity　**d.** stars

Key Words

Which one of the following words best suits each definition?

apparently / capture / current / fleeting / last

(1   ) : happening or existing now

(2   ) : lasting for a very short time

(3   ) : according to what you have heard or read; according to the way something appears

(4   ) : to continue for a particular period of time

(5   ) : to succeed in recording something in words or pictures

08 ナチュラル   09 ゆっくり〈ポーズなし〉   10 ゆっくり〈ポーズあり〉

 Listening

アメリカ英語

❖ Listen carefully and fill in the blanks.

Now, catching sight of a rainbow is always exciting–/ sometimes fleeting, only lasting a short amount of time;/ but, apparently, not in (1   ).// The Chinese Culture University says/ that they have captured a rainbow that lasted nearly nine hours,/ breaking a world record.// A professor there says/ his department is trying to collect more than (2   ) photographs/ to send to the Guinness World Records committee.// According to Reuters,/ the current record-holding rainbow was seen in the (3   )/ for at least six hours.// That was back in 1994.//

(December 5, 2017)

After listening

《 **True** 〈or〉 **False?** 》

(1) The Chinese Culture University succeeded in recording a rainbow that lasted for about nine hours.

(2) In 1994, a rainbow was seen for about six hours in the US.

✤ Choose the correct answer.

(1) Where was the longest-lasting rainbow on record observed?

    a. In Hong Kong.

    b. In mainland China.

    c. In Taiwan.

                       (   )

(2) Why is the Chinese Culture University trying to collect so many photographs of the rainbow?

    a. To prove how long it lasted.

    b. To show how beautiful it was.

    c. To write a scientific thesis on it.

                       (   )

observer ● 観察者、観測者

report ● 〜を報告する

catch sight of ... ● 〜を見かける、〜が目に入る

fleeting ● いつの間にか過ぎ去る、束の間の、はかない

last ● 続く、持続する

apparently ● どうやら〜らしい

capture ● 〜を（映像などに）捉える

break a record ● 記録を破る

department ● （組織における）部門、（大学の）学科

collect ● 〜を集める

Guinness World Records ● Guinness World Records 社は、毎年いわゆる『ギネスブック』(*The Guinness World Records*) を刊行している。

committee ● 委員会

current ● 現在の、現時点の

record-holding ● 記録を保持している

ここ、よく聴いてみて

2行目の **a short amount of time** のところの音の連鎖に注意してみてください。**short amount of** の3語がつながり、まるで1語みたい。最後の **of** の / v / の音は聞こえません。

3行目の **the Chinese Culture University** の **culture** は聞き取れましたか。/ l / の音で舌を上の歯の付け根に当て、そのまま「チャ」になだれこみ、「**カウ**チャ」のように聞こえます。

4行目の **nine hours** では **nine** ばかりでなく **hours** も強く、ゆっくり発音されているのに、8行目の **six hours** では **six** だけが強く発音されているのはなぜでしょう？

イディオムをもう1つ

「〜を見かける、〜を見つける」が catch sight of ... なら、視界にあったものを「見失う」は lose sight of ... です。これは日本語の「見失う」と同様、"Let's not lose sight of our original purpose."（もともとの目的を見失わないようにしましょう）のように比喩的にも使うことができます。

それから、諺の "Out of sight, out of mind." も覚えておきたい。直訳すれば、「視界から消えると念頭から去る」ですね。日本語の「去る者は日々に疎し」にそっくり。

Unit 4 Death of Chef Paul Bocuse

料理界の巨匠ポール・ボキューズ氏が死去

ウシ、ブタ、ヒツジは英語で言えますね。では、牛肉、豚肉、羊肉は？ そう、beef、pork、muttonです。これらは、それぞれウシ、ブタ、ヒツジの意のフランス語に由来します。今回出てくるchef, cuisine, restaurantといった語も、やはりフランス語起源。英語に入った時期は、beef、pork、muttonよりだいぶ遅いですけれど。

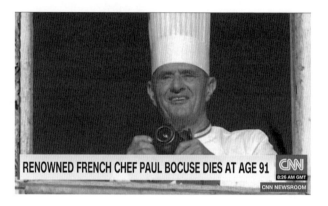

RENOWNED FRENCH CHEF PAUL BOCUSE DIES AT AGE 91

Before listening

❖ Choose the suitable words to fill in the blanks.

In 2010, the UN cultural organization (**1**   ) added traditional French cuisine to the world's (**2**   ) cultural heritage list. It was the first time that cuisine made it on to the list. Three years later, traditional Japanese food was also added to the list, along with (**3**   ) kimchi-making.

    (1)   a. ILO b. UNCTAD c. UNESCO d. WHO

    (2)   a. inaudible b. incredible c. intangible d. invisible

    (3)   a. China b. Chinese c. Korea d. Korean

Which one of the following words best suits each definition?

culinary / feast / icon / mentor / savvy

(1   ) : a famous person or thing that people see as a symbol of an important idea

(2   ) : a large or special meal where a lot of people celebrate an occasion

(3   ) : an experienced and trusted adviser who helps a less experienced person

(4   ) : having practical knowledge and ability

(5   ) : relating to cooking or food

ナチュラル　ゆっくり　ゆっくり
〈ポーズなし〉〈ポーズあり〉

アメリカ英語

✤ Listen carefully and fill in the blanks.

Legendary French chef Paul Bocuse is being remembered/ as a mentor, a savvy businessman,/ and a leading figure in transforming French cuisine.// Bocuse died Saturday at age (1   ).// He was an icon.// He became one of the first celebrity chefs,/ promoting French nouvelle cuisine around the world.// His international culinary empire/ began in his father's restaurant near (2   ).// Spanish American chef José Andrés paid tribute,/ writing on (3   ),/ "The angels will have a feast today./ Paul Bocuse has joined them."//

(January 21, 2018)

(1) Paul Bocuse was great both as a cook and as a businessperson.

(2) Paul Bocuse remained faithful to the traditions of French cooking.

❖ Choose the correct answer.

(1) Where did Paul Bocuse's international career begin?

    a. In America.

    b. In France.

    c. In Spain.

( )

(2) Why did José Andrés say the angels would have a feast that day?

    a. Because an annual festival was to be held for them to gather.

    b Because one of the greatest chefs on earth had joined them in heaven.

    c. Because they would come down to earth to try Bocuse's dishes.

( )

Notes

chef ● シェフ、料理長

legendary ● 伝説的な

remember ●（死者を）悼む、〜を追悼する

mentor ● 良き指導者

savvy ● 経験豊富な、実務に長けた

leading figure ● 第一人者

transform ● 変形させる、変貌させる、一変させる

cuisine ●（特定の地域などの）料理（法）

icon ● 象徴（的なもの、人）

celebrity ● 有名人（の）

promote ●（〜の販売を）促進する、（〜を）宣伝する

nouvelle cuisine ●〈仏〉ヌーベルキュイジーヌ、「新しい料理」

culinary ● 料理の

Lyon ● リヨン（フランス南東部の都市）

pay tribute ● 称賛の意を表する、弔意を表する

feast ● 祝宴、ごちそう

ここ、よく聴いてみて

　アメリカ英語なので、1行目の **mentor** は最後の **r** がよく響いています。

　4行目の **celebrity** は、**ce-leb-ri-ty** と4音節ですが、第2音節の **leb** に強勢が落ちたあとの2音節の発音は、かなりはしょられる感じ。

　最終行の **joined them** がまるで1語のようにつながって聞こえることにも注意してください。代名詞 **them** の **th** が直前の **d** と一体化し、**them** の母音 **e** も軽く / ə / と発音され、結果として「ヂョインダム」のように聞こえます。

イディオムをもう1つ

　今回は "Paul Bocuse has joined them [the angels]." という文で締めくくられましたので、join the majority（多数派に加わる）というイディオムを覚えておきましょう。これは、die（死ぬ）の婉曲語法（euphemism）です。現在、地上で生きているわたしたちより、すでに他界したご先祖様たちの数のほうがずっと多いというわけです。「他界」も一例ですが、死についての婉曲語法は英語にも日本語にもたくさんあります。ほかにどんなものがあるか調べてみてください。

Unit 5 KFC Runs Out of Chicken

英KFC、チキン不足で店舗大半が休業

英語の諺 "Don't count your chickens before they are hatched."（まだ孵らぬヒナを数えるな）をご存じですか。日本語の「とらぬ狸の皮算用（をするな）」にあたります。あれ？ なぜ、諺ではchickensと複数形なのに、今回のタイトルではsがつかないんでしょう？

From BBC/Monday
Bristol, England

FOWL PLAY: KFC IN UK RUNS OUT OF CHICKEN

CNN NEWSROOM

⬅ Before listening

✤ Choose the suitable words to fill in the blanks.

Domestication of the chicken dates back to at least (**1**　　) BC, and their ancestry can be traced back to four species of wild jungle fowl from Southeast (**2**　　). However, the red jungle fowl is the most commonly found wild species in the world today and is considered to be the main ancestor of the (**3**　　) chicken.

(1)　a. 500　b. 1000　c. 1500　d. 2000

(2)　a. Africa　b. Asia　c. Australia　d. Europe

(3)　a. domestic　b. fried　c. roast　d. wild

Key Words

Which one of the following words best suits each definition?

blame / feather / mix-up / ruffle / temporary

(1   ) : a mistake or misunderstanding that results in confusion

(2   ) : one of the many soft light parts that cover a bird's body

(3   ) : lasting for only a limited period of time; not permanent

(4   ) : to disturb the smooth surface of something, so that it is no longer even

(5   ) : to say or think that someone is responsible for a fault or mistake

14   15   16

ナチュラル ゆっくり ゆっくり
〈ポーズなし〉〈ポーズあり〉

オーストラリア英語

 **Listening**

♣ Listen carefully and fill in the blanks.

The fried-chicken restaurant chain KFC has egg on its face/ after temporarily closing 800 of its 900 locations in the United (**1**   ),/ because you can't run a chicken restaurant if you run out of chicken, of course.// There was no foul play involved,/ but a shipping problem (**2**   ) hundreds of KFC locations more than a little boneless and completely chickenless,/ as it were.// The company blames shipper (**3**   ) for the mix-up/ and hopes the temporary shutdown doesn't ruffle too many customers' feathers.//

(February 20, 2018)

 **After listening**

 **True or False?**

(1) KFC temporarily closed many of its locations in the United States.

(2) KFC's shortage of chicken was caused by some mistake, not by any wrongdoing.

✣ Choose the correct answer.

(1) How many restaurants does KFC have in Britain?

   a. Eight hundred.

   b. Nine hundred.

   c. More than nine hundred.

                                                                    (   )

(2) To what does KFC ascribe the chicken shortage?

   a. There being too many customers.

   b. There being too many restaurants.

   c. There having been a mistake in the shipping.

                                                                    (   )

Notes

KFC = Kentucky Fried Chicken
● ケンタッキーフライドチキン

run out of ... ● ～がなくなる、～を切らす

have egg on one's face
● 大恥をかく、笑い物になる

temporarily ● 一時的に、暫定的に

run ● ～を経営する、運営する

foul play
● 不正行為、犯罪行為 (p.18の画像のキャプションでは"fowl play"となっています。なぜでしょう？)

involve ● ～を含む、伴う

shipping ● 出荷、発送

more than a little ● 少なからず、かなり

boneless ● 骨のない、力強さを欠いた

as it were ● 言わば、言うなれば

blame A for B
● BをAのせいだと言う、BのことでAを責める

DHL ● ドイツの国際物流会社

mix-up
● 手違い、取り違え (の結果の混乱、ごたごた)

ruffle someone's feathers
● (人の) 感情を逆撫でする、(人を) 怒らせる

ここ、よく聴いてみて

　音の連鎖については、1行目の **egg on its** を注意して聞いてみてください。まるで1語のように聞こえます。

　最終行の **temporary** は、オーストラリア英語 (やイギリス英語) とアメリカ英語で発音がだいぶ違います。オーストラリア英語では、第1音節 の tem のところに強勢が落ち、そのあとは尻すぼまりになるのに対し、アメリカ英語では第3音節の ra に第2強勢が置かれるので聞き取りやすい。似たようなことは、例えば **library** という語でも起こります。アメリカ英語のほうが、ゆっくり、はっきりしている。

　1行目の **temporarily** も、オーストラリア英語 (やイギリス英語) では、第1音節に強勢が落ちたあとはムニャムニャッと終わってしまう。つまり、❶②③④⑤という感じ。これがアメリカ英語ですと、第1音節に軽く第2強勢を置き、第3音節の ra に第1強勢がきますから、聞き取りやすくなります。❶②❸④⑤という感じです。

　でも、今回、アメリカ英語とのいちばんわかりやすい違いは、3行目の **can't** が / kɑːnt / (カーント) と発音されていること。この長く伸ばす a の音は、Unit 7、12、14のイギリス英語でも出てきます。

イディオムをもう1つ

　ニワトリは臆病な動物ということになっています。ですから、"Don't be such a chicken!" (そんなにニワトリになるなよ) と言えば、「びくびくするな」ということ。動詞にして使った chicken out というイディオムもあり、"You're not chickening out, are you?" (おじけづいてやめるって言うんじゃないだろうな?) のように使います。

Unit 6

Pope Disallows Death Penalty

カトリック教会、死刑を容認せず

　日本語では「教皇」とか「法王」とか呼ぶローマ・カトリック教会最高位の聖職者のことを英語ではthe Popeと言います。これは「司教」(bishop) を意味するラテン語papaに由来し、そのラテン語papaの源には「父」(father) を意味するギリシャ語pappasがあります。

July 7
Bari, Italy

THE VATICAN IS NOW OFFICIALLY AGAINST THE DEATH PENALTY

@CNNBRK　EMMERSON MNANGAGWA DECLARED WINNER IN ZIMBABWE PRESIDENTIAL ELECTION

← Before listening

♣ Choose the suitable words to fill in the blanks.

Some (**1**　) people were executed in 20 countries in 2018, excluding China, a fall of 31 percent on 2017—when 993 deaths were recorded. (**2**　) International's review of the use of the death penalty, which was released in 2019, says that while the number of executions have fallen in some countries, several others have seen a rise, including the US, (**3**　), Singapore, South Sudan and Belarus.

(1)　**a.** 590　**b.** 690　**c.** 790　**d.** 890

(2)　**a.** Amnesty　**b.** Bird-Life　**c.** Lion Clubs　**d.** United Press

(3)　**a.** Japan　**b.** Mexico　**c.** the Philippines　**d.** Portugal

Key Words

Which one of the following words best suits each definition?

abolish / disallow / opponent / penalty / vocal

(1   ) : a person who disagrees with something and tries to stop or change it

(2   ) : a punishment for breaking a law or rule

(3   ) : expressing strong opinions freely and with confidence

(4   ) : to officially refuse to accept something

(5   ) : to officially put an end to a practice, system, etc.

ナチュラル　ゆっくり　ゆっくり
〈ポーズなし〉〈ポーズあり〉

アメリカ英語

✤ Listen carefully and fill in the blanks.

Pope Francis has declared/ that the death penalty is never admissible.// This (**1**   ) positions the Vatican on the matter,/ adding the change to the teachings of the Catholic Church.// And the Vatican says/ (**2**   ) will work to abolish the death penalty worldwide.// Pope Francis has been a vocal opponent of the death penalty/ since he became leader of all Catholics worldwide.// A Vatican spokesman said/ the change was (**3**   ) for a long time.//

(August 3, 2018)

《True 〈or〉 False?》

(1) Much to everyone's surprise, Pope Francis declared the death penalty wrong in all circumstances.

(2) As head of the Roman Catholic Church, Pope Francis has always been clear about his opposition to the death penalty.

❖ Choose the correct answer.

(1) What did Pope Francis change when he declared the death penalty unacceptable?

    a. Catholic Church doctrine.

    b. His way of thinking.

    c. The Bible.

                                           ( )

(2) What did the Vatican promise to do after Pope Francis's declaration?

    a. To preach Christianity all over the world.

    b. To try to end capital punishment globally.

    c. To make its position clear on the death penalty.

                                           ( )

Notes

pope ● ローマ教皇

disallow ● 〜を許さない、禁ずる

death penalty ● 死刑

admissible ● 容認可能な、許容できる

position ● 〜を位置づける、〜の立場を定める

the Vatican ● ヴァチカン (宮殿) 、ローマ教皇庁

matter ● 事柄、問題

add A to B ● AをBに加える

teachings ● (宗教などの) 教え、教義 (この意味では複数形で用いることが多い)

the Catholic Church ● カトリック教会

work to do ● 〜するべく努力する

abolish ● 〜を廃止する、撤廃する

worldwide ● 世界中で、世界的に

vocal ● 声高な、遠慮なく主張する

opponent ● 反対者

Catholic ● カトリック教徒

spokesman ● (男性の) 報道官、スポークスマン

ここ、よく聴いてみて

　今回のキーワード death penalty の中の penalty の音に慣れましょう。日本語の「ペ・ナ・ル・ティー」とはだいぶ違いますね。最初の「ペ」が強く、はっきり発音され、あとは弱く、すばやく発音される。つまり、❶②③という感じです。「ペ」以外のところの母音はあいまいで、「ナ」は「ヌ」に近くなっています。

　日本語で「バ・チ・カ・ン」とか「ヴァ・チ・カ・ン」とか言う Vatican も、頭の「ヴァ」に強勢が落ちます。「チ」のところの t の音がやわらかくなって、d のようにも r のようにも聞こえる。2行目の matter の中の t の音にも同じことが起こっています。Vatican とか matter とか、母音と母音の間にある t に生じやすい現象です。

イディオムをもう1つ

　相手に何かを聞かれて、答えは当然イエス、わかりきってるじゃないというとき、"Is the Pope Catholic?" と問い返す答え方があります。ローマ教皇はカトリックに決まっているからです。"Are you hungry?" "Is the Pope Catholic?" (「お腹へった?」「当然」) という具合に使う。類似の表現に、"Does a bear shit in the woods?" というのもありますが、ちょっと下品ですか？　"Is Bill Gates rich?" というのもあります。

Unit 7 New Zealand's "First Baby" at the UN

NZ首相が生後３カ月の娘と国連総会に出席

みなさん、FLOTUS（フロウタス）というのが何の頭字語 (acronym) か、ご存じですか。ヒント──POTUS（ポウタス）は President Of The United States です。これにならえば、今回の話題は FBONZ です。フボンズ？ いいづらいですね、これは。

AFP/Getty Images

NEW ZEALAND'S "FIRST BABY"
INFANT ATTENDS U.N. GENERAL ASSEMBLY
CNN
S&P ASX ▼ -1.00
CNN NEWSROOM

◀ Before listening

♣ Choose the suitable words to fill in the blanks.

In (1   ), New Zealand became the first country to give all adult women the right to vote in national elections. In 2018, New Zealand Prime Minister Jacinda Ardern became only the (2   ) prime minister to give birth while in office. The first such leader was Benazir Bhutto, prime minister of (3   ), who gave birth to her daughter in 1990.

(1)　a. 1793　b. 1828　c. 1893　d. 1928

(2)　a. first　b. second　c. third　d. fourth

(3)　a. Bangladesh　b. Cambodia　c. India　d. Pakistan

Key Words

Which one of the following words best suits each definition?

> assembly / delight / mock / note / tiny

(1   ) : a group of people gathered together for a common purpose

(2   ) : not real, but very similar

(3   ) : very small in size or amount

(4   ) : to give someone great pleasure and enjoyment

(5   ) : to mention something in order to draw attention to it

20 ナチュラル   21 ゆっくり〈ポーズなし〉   22 ゆっくり〈ポーズあり〉

イギリス英語

Listening

♣ Listen carefully and fill in the blanks.

Back to the UN,/ where a tiny visitor helped make history/ on (1   ).// New Zealnd Prime Minister Jacinda Ardern became the first female leader/ to bring a newborn to the General Assembly.// Ardern's (2   )-month-old daughter was given a mock security pass/ that listed her as the "First Baby" of New Zealand.// The UN was delighted to see the little one in the General Assembly Hall.// A spokesman noted/ that just (3   ) percent of the world's leaders are women/ and that the organization needs to make them as welcome as possible.//

(September 25, 2018)

《 True 〈or〉 False? 》

(1) New Zealand Prime Minister Jacinda Ardern brought her newborn baby to the UN Security Council.

(2) The UN representatives raised their eyebrows when they saw Jacinda Ardern's baby in the General Assembly Hall.

♣ Choose the correct answer.

(1) **Why did the United Nations give the First Baby of New Zealand a security pass?**

    a. To maintain tight security at the UN.

    b. To make the historic occasion enjoyable.

    c. To respond to New Zealand Prime Minister's request.

                                                (   )

(2) **What did a UN spokesman say the UN needs to do?**

    a. To create a special organization to promote gender balance in politics.

    b. To make the United Nations a comfortable place for female leaders of the world.

    c. To organize a worldwide campaign in support of female politicians.

                                                (   )

UN = United Nations ● 国際連合、国連

tiny ● とても小さい

visitor ● 訪問者

make history ● 歴史に残ることをする、歴史を変える

prime minister ● 首相

newborn = newborn baby ● 新生児

General Assembly = UN General Assembly ● (国連) 総会

mock ● にせの、まがいものの、模造の

security pass ● 入場許可証

list A as B ● AをBとして挙げる

be delighted to do ● 〜して大喜びする

little one ● 小さな人、子ども

General Assembly Hall = UN General Assembly Hall ● (国連) 本会議場

note that ... ● (注意を引くために) 〜と発言する、〜ということを指摘する

make ... welcome ● 〜を温かく迎える、〜を歓迎する

ここ、よく聴いてみて

　イギリス英語の特徴の1つは、ask や bath や chance や father に現れる / ɑː / (アー) と口を大きく開いて長く伸ばす a の音。今回は、security pass (入場許可証) の pass がその例です。「パース」と発音されていますね。これらの a は、アメリカ英語では bag や cat や hat と同じように、短く / æ / と発音されます。

　特徴のもう1つは、語末の r が発音されないこと。今回なら、visitor、minister、leader、daughter に気をつけてみてください。leader は / líːdə / (リーダ) となります。

　音の連鎖の観点からは、最後の文にある make them as welcome as possible の最初の3語 make them as のところ、つながってまるで1語みたいに聞こえます。

イディオムをもう1つ

　今回は、make history が出てきましたから、go down in history というのも覚えておきましょう。"Ardern made history on Monday." とほぼ同じことを、"What she did on Monday will go down in history." ということができます。ちょっとだけ、使い方が違うようですね。

Unit **8** Rare Appearance of "Living Goddess"

ネパールの生き女神「クマリ」が祝祭に登場

「女神」を意味する goddess は、女性を表す接尾辞の -ess を god（神）に付けたことばです。類例に、princess（王女）、lioness（雌ライオン）、tigress（雌トラ）など。でも、この -ess を職業を表す語に付けた actress や authoress や poetess は時代遅れ。今は、性別を問わず、actor、author、poet を使うのが普通です。

Monday
Kathmandu, Nepal

NEPAL DEITY
"LIVING GODDESS" MAKES RARE APPEARANCE

◀ Before listening

♣ Choose the suitable words to fill in the blanks.

The Nepal Himalaya is the most formidable mountain range in the world, with nearly a (**1**   ) of the country lying above the elevation of 3,500 m. Eight of the world's highest peaks, including Mt. Everest, lie within Nepal's territory, which are all over (**2**   ) above sea level. Everest was first climbed by Edmund Hillary and Tenzing Norgay in (**3**   ) with a British expedition led by John Hunt.

(**1**)   a. fifth   b. quarter   c. third   d. half

(**2**)   a. 5,000 m   b. 6,000 m   c. 7,000 m   d. 8,000 m

(**3**)   a. 1913   b. 1933   c. 1953   d. 1973

Key Words

Which one of the following words best suits each definition?

deity / mortal / puberty / rare / relinquish

(1   ) : a god or goddess

(2   ) : a human being subject to death

(3   ) : the stage in life when you start to become physically
                mature

(4   ) : not happening very often

(5   ) : to stop having something; to give something up

23 ナチュラル 24 ゆっくり〈ポーズなし〉 25 ゆっくり〈ポーズあり〉

 Listening

オーストラリア英語

✤ Listen carefully and fill in the blanks.

Well,/ crowds in Kathmandu recently got a (**1**   ) chance to see a "living goddess."// The young deity made her (**2**   ) public appearance/ at a festival in Nepal.// Living goddesses are young girls who are chosen from the local community/ and live most of the time in temples.// They're (**3**   ) seen,/ except on special occasions.// When one reaches puberty,/ she must relinquish her position/ and go back to living with us mere mortals.//

(September 26, 2018)

 **After listening**

 **True or False?**

(1) People in Kathmandu seldom catch sight of a "living goddess."

(2) Living goddesses are young girls who come from all over Nepal.

✤ Choose the correct answer.

(1) Where do the living goddesses mostly spend their time?

    a. At home.

    b. In temples.

    c. In the mountains.

                                      (   )

(2) What happens to living goddesses when they reach puberty?

    a. A festival is held to celebrate their puberty.

    b. They leave home.

    c. They return to normal life.

                                        (   )

Notes

rare ● まれな、珍しい

appearance ● 出現、登場

living goddess ● 生き女神

crowd ● 群衆、人込み

Kathmandu ● カトマンズ (ネパールの首都)

deity ● (多神教の) 神、女神

make an appearance ● 姿を現す、出現する

local community ● 地元の共同体 (市町村)

temple ● 寺院

except on special occasions ● 特別な場合を除いて

puberty ● 思春期

relinquish ● ～を放棄する

position ● 地位、身分

mere mortal ● (神ならぬ身の) ただの人間

ここ、よく聴いてみて

　今回はオーストラリア英語。その特徴が出ているのは、2行目の deity と5行目の seen です。/ iː / (イー) の音がちょっと癖のある発音になっているのがわかりますか。「ディーイティ」は「デーエティ」に、「スィーン」は「セーン」に近づいています。

　なお、アンカーパーソンは goddess の第2音節に強勢を置いて発音していますが (①❷)、タイトル中の goddess の発音のように第1音節に強勢を置くのが普通です (❶②)。

イディオムをもう1つ

　やや古めかしい日本語に「銀幕の女王」ということばがありますが、それに相当する英語は a screen goddess です。もちろん、「女王」も goddess も比喩 (metaphor)。ストレートにいえば、a female film [movie] star となります。あ、star も比喩でした。

　ついでですから、「銀盤の女王」にあたる the queen of the ice も覚えておきましょうか。

Unit 9 Adventurer Swims around Britain

イギリス本島沿岸を陸に上がらず泳いで一周

　イギリスもイタリアほどではありませんが長靴っぽい格好をしています。その長靴のつま先にあたる岬の名をLand's Endといいます。逆にブリテン島の最北端とされているのはJohn o'Groatsという村。それで、"from John o'Groats to Land's End"（英国の北から南まで）という決まり文句があります。両地点間は道路距離にして約1,400キロです。

Sunday
Margate, England

EPIC SWIM
ADVENTURER COMPLETES SWIM AROUND BRITAIN
CNN
1:42 AM CET
@HolmesCNN

 Before listening

❖ Choose the suitable words to fill in the blanks.

During his tour of the United States, after a failed attempt to climb Mt. Everest, (1　　) was famously asked why he was attempting to scale the world's highest peak. He is said to have replied, "Because it's (2　　)." These words have been repeated by adventurers of all types to (3　　) their objective.

(1)　a. Edmund Hillary　b. David Livingstone
　　　c. George Mallory　d. Robert Peary

(2)　a. beautiful　b. impossible　c. mine　d. there

(3)　a. achieve　b. declare　c. justify　d. specify

Key Words

Which one of the following words best suits each definition?

| complete / current / emerge / equivalent / feat |

(1   ) : an achievement that needs great courage, skill or strength

(2   ) : the movement of water in the sea, a river, etc.

(3   ) : having the same value, amount, importance, etc.

(4   ) : to finish doing or making something

(5   ) : to appear or come out from somewhere

26 ナチュラル

27 ゆっくり 〈ポーズなし〉

28 ゆっくり 〈ポーズあり〉

Listening

アメリカ英語

❖ Listen carefully and fill in the blanks.

Jellyfish, salt water, powerful currents, and almost 3,000 kilometers of open water—/ but this British adventurer would not be stopped.//
(1   )-year-old Ross Edgley emerged from the sea/ at Margate, England, Sunday,/ to become the first person to swim around Britain.// Edgley spent five months/ swimming up to 12 hours a day/ to complete the (2   )-kilometer feat.// And, oh,/ that was after/ he climbed a rope equivalent to the height of Mt. (3   )/ and ran a marathon pulling a car.// Really?// Is he human?//

(November 5, 2018)

《 True ◇ or ◇ False? 》

(1)   Ross Edgley completed his swim around Britain at Margate, England.

(2)   Ross Edgley swam 12 hours every day to accomplish his
2,800-kilometer feat.

✤ Choose the correct answer.

(1)   How long did it take Ross Edgley to swim around Britain?

   a. Less than half a year.

   b. Less than a third of a year.

   c. Less than a quarter of a year.

(   )

(2)   Which of the following feats had Ross Edgley performed?

   a. Climbing Mt. Everest.

   b. Pulling a car for 42.195 kilometers.

   c. Skiing to the North Pole.

(   )

adventurer ● 冒険家

Britain = Great Britain ● (大) ブリテン島

jellyfish ● クラゲ

salt water ● 塩水、海水

current ● 流れ、潮流、海流

open water ● (陸地や氷に閉ざされていない) 開けた水域

emerge from ... ● 〜から出てくる、現れる

Margate ● マーゲイト (イングランド南東部の海浜保養地)

spend ... doing ● (時間) を〜して過ごす

up to ... ● 最大 [最長、最高] 〜まで

complete ● 〜を完遂する、完了する

feat ● 離れ業、偉業

equivalent to ... ● 〜と同等 [同量、同価値] の

run a marathon ● マラソンを走る

ここ、よく聴いてみて

　今回2度出てくる water の音に注意してみてください。t の音が t らしくないと思いませんか。特に2行目の open water のほう。t よりやわらかい d のような r のような音になっています。このように、強勢のある母音と強勢のない母音にはさまれた t (つまり、butter や party や writing などの中の t) が軟化するのはアメリカ英語の特徴の1つ。この現象、Unit 6 にも出てきました。

　ついでに申し上げておくと、同じ条件下の d にも同じことが起こります。例えば、wedding とかですね。

イディオムをもう1つ

　今回は "Is he human?" で締めくくられていました。この人、超人？　それとも神？　というわけです。逆に、あの人も神様じゃないからね、ただの人間だからね、間違えることもあるさ、というようなときは、"He's only human." といいます。諺も覚えておきましょうか。"To err is human; to forgive, divine." (過つは人の常、許すは神の業)

Unit 10 Emperor's Final New Year's Speech

天皇陛下最後の新年一般参賀に14万人超が参列

　日本国憲法によって「象徴」と規定された天皇が「君主」(monarch) であるか否かという憲法学上の論争はさておき、世界では日本を英国と同様に「立憲君主国」(constitutional monarchy) と捉えるのが普通です。日本を「共和国」(republic) の範疇に入れるのは難しいのでしょう。

ROYAL ABDICATION
JAPAN'S EMPEROR MAKES FINAL NEW YEAR'S APPEARANCE

✣ Choose the suitable words to fill in the blanks.

In April 2011, just before the Royal Wedding of Prince William and Catherine Middleton, a poll found that 75% of the public would like Britain to remain a (**1**　　), with 18% in favor of Britain becoming a (**2**　　). In May 2012, just before the Queen's (**3**　　) Jubilee, 80% were in favor of the (**1**　　), with 13% in favor of the United Kingdom becoming a (**2**　　). This was a record high figure in recent years in favor of the (**1**　　).

- (1)　a. monarch　b. monarchy　c. republic　d. republican
- (2)　a. monarch　b. monarchy　c. republic　d. republican
- (3)　a. Silver　b. Ruby　c. Golden　d. Diamond

Key Words

Which one of the following words best suits each definition?

> abdicate / adore / era / monarch / reign

(1   ) : a king, queen, or emperor

(2   ) : a period of time in history

(3   ) : the period of rule of a king, queen, emperor, etc.

(4   ) : to give up the position of being king, queen, or emperor

(5   ) : to love and respect someone deeply

🎧 Listening

29 ナチュラル　30 ゆっくり〈ポーズなし〉　31 ゆっくり〈ポーズあり〉

アメリカ英語

♣ Listen carefully and fill in the blanks.

An end of an era in Japan:/ Emperor Akihito will step down from the throne in April,/ ending his three-decade reign.// The (1   )-year-old royal delivered his final New Year's speech on Wednesday,/ saying that he is praying for world peace.// A record crowd—/ more than (2   ) people—/ reportedly came to greet the monarch at the Imperial Palace.// The widely adored emperor/ will be the first to abdicate in more than (3   ) centuries.//

(January 2, 2019)

⬇ After listening

《 True ‹or› False? 》

(1) Emperor Akihito is abdicating after 30 years as Japan's monarch.

(2) More than 100,000 people came to the Imperial Palace to pay their respects to Emperor Akihito.

❖ Choose the correct answer.

(1) What did Emperor Akihito say he was praying for?

    a. For peace in the world.

    b. For the souls of the war dead.

    c. For the victims of a natural disaster.

(   )

(2) How many years was it since an emperor last abdicated the throne?

    a. Over three hundred years.

    b. Over two hundred years.

    c. Over one hundred years.

(   )

Notes

emperor ● 皇帝、(日本の) 天皇

era ● 時代

throne ● 玉座、王位、(日本の) 皇位

decade ● 10年

reign ● 治世、在位期間

royal ● 王室 [皇室] の人

deliver ● (演説などを) 行う

pray for ... ● 〜を求めて祈る

record ● 記録的な

reportedly ● 伝えられるところによると

greet ● 〜にあいさつする

monarch ● 君主

the Imperial Palace ● 皇居

adore ● 〜を敬愛する

abdicate ● 退位する

ここ、よく聴いてみて

　今回は2つの副詞 **reportedly** (5行目) と **widely** (6行目) に注意してみてください。このように **d** と **l** がつながると、**d** の音をはじかずに、そのまま **l** の音に流れていくことが少なくありません。結果として、「リ**ポー**テッ (ル) リィ」「**ワイ (ル)** リィ」のような感じになる。類例に、**candle** (「**キャン** (ル) ル」)、**middle** (「**ミ (ル)** ル」) など。

　同様の現象は、**t** と **l** がつながったときも起こります。例えば、**exactly** や **bottle** の **t** が呑み込まれる感じで、「イグ**ザク** (ル) リィ」「**ボ (ル)** ル」のように聞こえます。

イディオムをもう1つ

　1〜2行目の step down from the throne は文字どおりには「玉座から下りる」ですが、比喩的に「王位を退く」の意になります。「王位につく」は come to the throne、「王位にある」は be on the throne です。

　また、step down のもう1つの使い方に、step down as prime minister (首相を辞任する) があります。役職名がくるときは as になるのですね。

Unit **11** Better Investment with Gender Balance

チームの男女バランスが収益に影響？

なぜ、釣り合い（がとれていること）を「バランス」というのでしょう。てんびん座の方はご存じかもしれませんね。そう、英語のbalanceのもともとの意味は「てんびん」なのです。てんびん座のことは、the BalanceまたはLibra（これはラテン語で「てんびん」）またはthe Scales（scaleはてんびんに2つあるお皿のこと）といいます。

GENDER BALANCE STUDY

10 to 20% higher returns

INTERNATIONAL WOMEN'S DAY — LIVE

STUDY: FUNDS WITH GENDER-BALANCED LEADERSHIP DO BETTER — CNN

Private equity and venture capital funds generated 10-20% higher returns — DAX ▲ 15.15

← Before listening

❖ Choose the suitable words to fill in the blanks.

In 2019, Chizuko Ueno, a sociologist and prominent (**1**   ) figure in Japan, gave a speech at the University of Tokyo entrance ceremony. She pointed out that less than (**2**   ) percent of students entering the University of Tokyo are female, despite there being plentiful evidence that female applicants have (**3**   ) academic scores than their male competitors.

(1) **a.** alpinist **b.** feminist **c.** nationalist **d.** pacifist

(2) **a.** 20 **b.** 30 **c.** 40 **d.** 50

(3) **a.** closer **b.** higher **c.** lower **d.** similar

Key Words

Which one of the following words best suits each definition?

> evidence / generate / gender / investment / return

(1   ) : facts that show that something is true

(2   ) : males or females, considered as a social and cultural group

(3   ) : the profit that you get from economic activities

(4   ) : the use of money in the hope of making a profit

(5   ) : to produce or create

ナチュラル　ゆっくり　ゆっくり
〈ポーズなし〉〈ポーズあり〉

Listening

アメリカ英語

✤ Listen carefully and fill in the blanks.

There's new evidence/ that, in business, it's (**1**   ) to have both men and women on the team.// Now, a new study by the International Finance Corporation,/ a member of the World Bank Group,/ looked at private-equity and venture-capital funds.// It found/ that performance with gender-balanced senior investment teams/ generated 10 to even up to 20 percent (**2**   ) returns,/ as (**3**   ) with funds that had a majority of male or female leaders.// So it's all about the balance.//

(March 7, 2019)

43

⟪ True ⟨or⟩ False? ⟫

(1) New evidence has been found that gender balance does matter in business.

(2) A new study of gender balance in business was conducted by the World Bank.

❖ Choose the correct answer.

(1) What is found to be influenced by the male/female ratio of an investment team?

    a. The profit it makes.

    b. The sense of fulfillment its members feel.

    c. The type of social issues it solves.

                             ( )

(2) As far as the returns it yields are concerned, how does a gender-balanced investment team compare with an imbalanced one?

    a. More than 20 percent better.

    b. Between 10 and 20 percent better.

    c. Approximately 10 percent better.

                             ( )

Notes

investment ● 投資

gender balance ● 男女数のバランス (本文5行目のgender-balancedは「男女数のバランスのとれた」という形容詞)

evidence that ... ● 〜ということを示す証拠

study ● 調査、研究

International Finance Corporation ● 国際金融公社

World Bank Group ● 世界銀行グループ

look at ... ● 〜を調べる、検討する

private equity ● 未公開株式 (本文ではハイフンで結んで形容詞にしている)

venture capital ● 冒険資本 (本文ではハイフンで結んで形容詞にしている)

fund ● 基金、資金

performance ● (投資における) 運用実績

senior team ● 幹部、上層部

generate ● 生み出す

up to ... ● 最大 [最長、最高] 〜まで

return ● 利益、収益 (この意味では、しばしば複数形)

majority ● 大多数、大半

it's all about ... ● 肝心なのは〜である

ここ、よく聴いてみて

2行目の **international** と6行目の 20 (**twenty**) で同じような音の変化が起こっていることに気がつきますか。ええ、**n** のあとの **t** ですね。**n** にひきずられて **t** も **n** に近づいている。「インナ**ナ**ショナル」「**トゥエンニィ**」みたいな感じになっています。ほかにも、**plenty** (**プレンニィ**) や **intersection** (インナ**セク**ション) など。これはアメリカ英語の発音の特徴です。

イディオムをもう1つ

1〜2行目の have both men and women on the team の前置詞 on は覚えておきましょう。誰かが「チームに入っている、チームの一員だ」なら be on the team となります。例えば、エリカさんが大学のバスケットボールチームに入っているのなら、"Erica is on the university basketball team." といいます。

この on は、team のほかにも、committee (委員会)、jury (陪審団)、panel (パネル、専門家集団)、staff (スタッフ、職員) などの一員だ、というときにも使えます。

Unit 12 Taiwan's First Same-Sex Marriages

アジア初、台湾が同性婚を合法化

同性愛を意味するhomosexualityのhomo-は「同一の」の意の連結形。異性愛を意味するheterosexualityのhetero-は「他の、異なった」の意の連結形。両性愛を意味するbisexualityのbi-は「二つの、両方の」の意の連結形です。では、トランスジェンダーのtrans は？

LGBTQ EQUALITY

FIRST COUPLES WED UNDER TAIWAN'S MARRIAGE EQUALITY LAW

CNN NEWSROOM

◀ Before listening

♣ Choose the suitable words to fill in the blanks.

In Ireland, it became legal for same-sex couples to marry in 2015. Irish Prime Minister Leo Varadkar, who is (**1**) gay, said in a speech in front of Pope Francis during his visit to Ireland in 2018, "The Ireland of the (**2**) century is a very different place today than it was in the past. Ireland is increasingly (**3**)."

(1) a. open   b. openly   c. secret   d. secretly

(2) a. 20st   b. 20th   c. 21st   d. 21th

(3) a. diverse   b. diversity   c. intolerance   d. intolerant

Key Words

Which one of the following words best suits each definition?

> bill / continent / equality / gay / groundbreaking

(1   ) : a situation in which people have the same rights, status, advantages, etc.

(2   ) : a very large land mass surrounded by sea

(3   ) : a written proposal for a new law that is presented to a parliament for discussion

(4   ) : involving making new discoveries and using new methods

(5   ) : sexually attracted to people of one's own sex

ナチュラル　ゆっくり　ゆっくり
〈ポーズなし〉〈ポーズあり〉

イギリス英語

Listening

❖ Listen carefully and fill in the blanks.

It's a historic day in Taiwan,/ because same-sex couples there can now get married.// This is one of the (1   ) gay couples—/ that you're going to be looking at now—/ in (2   ) of Asia to be legally wed.// Taiwan's groundbreaking marriage equality bill/ is now in effect,/ a week after it was passed.// Activists hope/ it will spark change across the (3   ) continent,/ though some countries are rolling back LGBTQ rights.//

(May 24, 2019)

 **After listening**

 **True** or **False?**

(1) Taiwan has become the first country in the world to legalize same-sex marriage.

(2) Some countries are experiencing negative reactions to increased LGBTQ rights.

❖ Choose the correct answer.

(1) How long did it take Taiwan's marriage-equality bill to come into effect after it was passed?

    a. A week.

    b. A month.

    c. A year.

(   )

(2) What do activists want to see after Taiwan legalized same-sex marriage?

    a. A change in the attitude of Taiwanese people.

    b. A change of leadership in Taiwan.

    c. A policy change in other Asian countries.

(   )

same-sex ● 同性（間）の

historic ● 歴史的な

get married ● 結婚する

gay ● 同性愛（者）の

legally ● （合）法的に；法律上

wed ● ～を結婚させる（本文中のwedは過去分詞）

groundbreaking ● 画期的な、革新的な

marriage-equality bill ● 婚姻に関する平等を定める法案

be in effect ● 効力を有して、（法律が）施行されて

pass ● （法案を）通過させる、可決する

activist ● 活動家

spark ● ～を引き起こす、誘発する

continent ● 大陸（ここではthe continentでアジア大陸を指す）

roll back ● ～を押し返す、後退させる

LGBTQ
= lesbian, gay, bisexual, transgender, and questioning or queer

right ● 権利

ここ、よく聴いてみて

　音の連鎖で注意したいのは、3行目の you're going to be looking at now のところ。ずいぶん早口ですね。特に、**going to** はまとめて / gɔnə / （ゴナ）と発音されている。この「ゴナ」と発音される **going to** は、例えば小説などで、文字の上でも **gonna** と表記されることがあります。

　イギリス英語の特徴としては、Unit 7でもお話しした / ɑː / （アー）と長く伸ばす **a** の音を5行目の **after** と **passed** に聞くことができます。

イディオムをもう1つ

　今回出てきたgroundbreakingという形容詞のもとにあるのは、break groundというイディオムです。文字どおりには「土を起こす、耕す、土地を開拓する」の意、比喩的には「新生面を開く、新分野に踏み出す」の意で使います。

　ついでに、blaze a trailも覚えておきましょう。これも比喩的に「新しい道を切り開く」の意。そこからtrailblazing（先駆的な、草分けの）という形容詞と、trailblazer（先駆者、草分け）という名詞ができました。

　なお、このblazeは「（樹木に）目印の傷をつける」という意味の動詞で、「炎」の意の名詞（また「燃え立つ」の意の動詞）であるblazeとは、同じ綴りですが、別の語です。

Unit 13

Alabama Gets Strict Abortion Law

米アラバマ州で厳しい中絶禁止法が成立

　アメリカ合衆国という連邦 (federal union) を構成する50の「州」は英語では "state" (国家) です。それぞれ独立性が高く、州法 (state law) があって州憲法があり、州裁判所があって州最高裁判所がある。そして、ときどき、連邦最高裁判所 (＝合衆国最高裁判所) が州法を違憲 (unconstitutional) と判断することがあります。

Alabama Governor's Office

TARGETING ROE V. WADE
ALABAMA ADOPTS MOST RESTRICTIVE ABORTION LAW IN U.S.
CNN
KOSPI ▼ -25.09
CNN NEWSROOM

◀ Before listening

♣ Choose the suitable words to fill in the blanks.

In 1970, a Texas woman challenged the (**1**   ) law that banned abortion, and her case eventually went to the US Supreme Court. The Court decided in 1973 that the constitutional right to (**2**   ) includes a woman's right to decide whether to have an abortion and that the Texas law was unconstitutional. However, Americans still remain (**3**   ) over a woman's right to choose an abortion.

(1)　**a.** town　**b.** county　**c.** state　**d.** federal

(2)　**a.** education　**b.** equality　**c.** privacy　**d.** vote

(3)　**a.** divided　**b.** ignorant　**c.** optimistic　**d.** united

Key Words

Which one of the following words best suits each definition?

advocate / appalling / legislation / precious / testament

(1   ) : a law or a set of laws; the process of making laws

(2   ) : a person who publicly supports someone or something

(3   ) : something that shows that something else exists or is true

(4   ) : extremely bad; shocking

(5   ) : of great value and importance

38 ナチュラル   39 ゆっくり〈ポーズなし〉   40 ゆっくり〈ポーズあり〉

 Listening

オーストラリア英語

❖ Listen carefully and fill in the blanks.

In Alabama,/ the governor has signed into law a bill/ that could punish doctors who perform abortions there with life in prison.// The law bans abortions (1   ) almost all cases,/ even for victims of rape and incest.// It is a move/ critics call an appalling attack (2   ) women's rights,/ and abortion-rights advocates promise to challenge it in court.// Republican governor Kay Ivey says,/ "This legislation stands as a powerful testament (3   ) Alabamians' deeply held belief/ that every life is precious."//

(April 28, 2019)

After listening

«True ‹or› False?»

(1) Under the new law, abortion is illegal in Alabama, except for victims of rape and incest.

(2) Kay Ivey, Governor of Alabama, is a member of the Republican Party.

✤ Choose the correct answer.

(1) What kind of punishment could doctors in Alabama face for performing abortions?

    a. A life sentence.

    b. Capital punishment.

    c. No more than fines.

        ( )

(2) What do pro-choice advocates plan to do about the new Alabama state law?

    a. Send a petition to the President.

    b. Take legal action against it.

    c. Hold mass demonstrations on the streets.

        ( )

strict ● 厳格な、厳しい

abortion ● 妊娠中絶、堕胎

governor ● 知事

sign a bill into law ● 法案に署名して法律にする

punish ... with life in prison ● ～を終身刑に処する

perform ● （手術などを）行う

ban ● ～を禁止する

victim ● 犠牲者、被害者

incest ● 近親相姦

move ● 動き、行動、措置

critic ● 批判する人；批評家

appalling ● ぞっとするような、恐ろしい

advocate ● 擁護者、支持者

challenge ... in court ● ～に法廷で異議を申し立てる

Republican ● 共和党（員）の

legislation ● 立法；法律

stand as ... ● ～として存在する

testament to ... ● ～の証拠、証し

deeply held belief ● 固く信じている考え、信念

precious ● 貴重な、かけがえのない

ここ、よく聴いてみて

　全体にゆっくりと、1語1語はっきりと発音されていますね。そのため、1行目の the governor と a bill の冠詞 the と a が、それぞれ / ðíː / （ズィー）と / éɪ / （エイ）と強調気味に発音されています。

　アンカーパーソンがどんな語を特に強く、ゆっくり発音しているかに注意してみてください。

イディオムをもう1つ

　「法廷で」が in court なら、「法廷外で」は out of court です。「（その一件に）法廷で決着をつける」は settle (the matter) in court、「（その一件を）示談で解決する」は settle (the matter) out of court といいます。

　名詞にして an out-of-court settlement とすれば「示談、法廷外の和解」です。

Unit 14 Queen Elizabeth Gives Up Real Fur

女王のワードローブに「フェイク」が仲間入り

　「動物の倫理的扱いを求める人々の会」(PETA。/pí:tə/ (ピータ) と発音します) という、動物の権利 (animal rights) を擁護する団体をご存じですか。世界各地でキャンペーンを行い、ときに過激な活動で物議を醸すこともあります。食肉、動物実験、そして衣服への毛皮や皮革、羊毛、絹の使用に反対しています。

QUEEN ELIZABETH DITCHES REAL FUR FOR FAKE

 Before listening

✤ Choose the suitable words to fill in the blanks.

Speciesism is the idea that being human is a good enough reason for human beings to have greater rights than non-human animals. Speciesism is often criticized as the same sort of prejudice as (1   ) or sexism. People who (2   ) speciesism say that giving human beings greater rights than non-human animals is as (3   ) wrong as giving white people greater rights than non-white people.

(1)　a. capitalism　b. fatalism　c. racism　d. socialism

(2)　a. import　b. oppose　c. suppose　d. support

(3)　a. accidental　b. accidentally　c. moral　d. morally

Key Words

Which one of the following words best suits each definition?

authorized / ditch / engagement / fake / urge

(1   ) : an official arrangement to do something at a particular time

(2   ) : appearing to be something it is not; not genuine

(3   ) : having official permission or approval

(4   ) : to stop having something; to get rid of something

(5   ) : to strongly advise someone to do something

ナチュラル　ゆっくり　ゆっくり
〈ポーズなし〉〈ポーズあり〉

 **Listening**

イギリス英語

❖ Listen carefully and fill in the blanks.

This winter season,/ Queen Elizabeth has ditched fur.// That's according to the queen's senior dresser, Angela (**1**   ),/ who writes in her authorized book:/ "If Her Majesty is due to attend an engagement/ in particularly cold weather,/ from (**2**   ) onwards,/ fake fur will be used to make sure she stays warm."// It comes (**3**   ) years after the animal-rights group PETA urged the queen/ to get with these more enlightened times.//

(November 6, 2019)

After listening

« True or False? »

(1) Queen Elizabeth herself announced that she would quit wearing real fur

(2) In 2013, the animal-rights group PETA called on Queen Elizabeth to go fur-free.

❖ Choose the correct answer.

(1) What does Angela Kelly do?

    a. She is an animal-rights activist.

    b. She is responsible for what Queen Elizabeth wears.

    c. She writes books.

( )

(2) What will Queen Elizabeth do from 2019 onwards when she is scheduled to go out on a freezing day?

    a. Cancel the appointment.

    b. Put off the appointment.

    c. Put on fake fur.

( )

Notes

give up ●	(習慣などを) やめる、断つ
fur ●	毛皮
ditch ●	(口語) 〜を捨てる、〜をやめる
be according to ... ●	(情報源は) 〜である
senior ●	(地位について) 上級の、上位の
dresser ●	衣装係
authorized ●	公認された、許可を得た
Her Majesty ●	女王陛下 (女王や国王の配偶者に対する敬称。3人称)
be due to do ●	〜する予定である
attend ●	〜に出席する
engagement ●	約束、予定、用事

particularly ●	特に、とりわけ
from ... onwards ●	〜以降
fake ●	にせの、模造の
make sure (that) ... ●	確実に〜となるようにする
animal-rights group ●	動物の権利擁護団体
PETA = People for the Ethical Treatment of Animals	
urge ... to do ●	…に〜するよう促す
get with the times ●	時代に遅れずついていく
enlightened ●	啓蒙された、文明の進んだ

ここ、よく聴いてみて

　イギリス英語やオーストラリア英語では、**rain** のように母音の前にある **r** は発音しますが、それ以外の **r** は発音しません。今回ですと、**winter, fur, according, senior, dresser, her, particularly, weather, onwards, warm, years, after, urge** の中の **r** が発音されません。(**dresser** の中の最初の **r** は、母音の前の **r** ですから発音されます)。これらのrを響かせるアメリカ英語とはだいぶ印象が変わってきます。例えば、**winter** は / wíntə / (**ウィンタ**) となり、アメリカ英語と比べると短くて、よく言えばサッパリした、悪く言えばちょっとそっけない感じ。

　また、**after** には Unit 7と12でもお話しした、これもイギリス英語の特徴である「アー」と長く伸ばす **a** の音も出てきて、/ ɑ́:ftə / (**アーフタ**) となります。

イディオムをもう1つ

　「時代に遅れずついていく」の get with the times の get の代わりに move や change や keep up が入ることも多いので頭に入れておいてください。

　このうちの keep up with ... というのは、「(一緒に歩いている人に) 遅れずについていく」というのが文字どおりの意味。「(先を行く人に) 追いつく」の意の catch up with ... とペアにして覚えておきましょう。

　ところで、keep up with the Joneses (ジョーンズ家の人たちに遅れずついていく) という決まり文句もあります。どんな意味だか想像がつきますか？

各ユニットの "Choose the suitable words to fill in the blanks." (Before Listening) の英文は、ここに示した記事等に適宜修正を加えて作成したものです。

Unit 1: Void Found in Giza's Great Pyramid
"Jīzah, Al- or Giza". Britannica Concise Encyclopedia.

Unit 2: Railway Apologizes for 20-Second Error
"Rail transport in Great Britain".
 https://en.wikipedia.org/wiki/Rail_transport_in_Great_Britain.
Glyn Williams. *"Railways in Japan".*
https://www.sinfin.net/railways/world/japan/index.html.

Unit 3: Observers Report Nine-Hour Rainbow
"All the colours of the rainbow".
https://www.bbc.co.uk/programmes/articles/21mSPZS58ITyryYNcKTxJrf/all-the-colours-of-the-rainbow.

Unit 4: Death of Chef Paul Bocuse
"French gastronomy recognised by UN culture body".
https://www.bbc.com/news/world-11768231.
"Japanese cuisine added to Unesco 'intangible heritage' list".
https://www.bbc.com/news/av/world-asia-25223105/japanese-cuisine-added-to-unesco-intangible-heritage-list.

Unit 5: KFC Runs Out of Chicken
"History of the Chicken".
https://extension.psu.edu/history-of-the-chicken.

Unit 6: Pope Disallows Death Penalty
"Global executions fall to lowest level in a decade, Amnesty says".
https://www.bbc.com/news/world-47867201.

Unit 7: New Zealand's "First Baby" at the UN
"Women's right to vote".
https://www.bbc.co.uk/learningenglish/features/6-minute-english/ep-161124.
"Ardern and Bhutto: Two different pregnancies in power".
https://www.bbc.com/news/world-asia-44568537.

Unit 8: Rare Appearance of "Living Goddess"
"Mountaineering in Nepal".
https://www.welcomenepal.com/things-to-do/mountaineering.html.

Unit 9: Adventurer Swims around Britain
Stacy Bare. *"What Everest Climber Really Meant by 'Because It's There'".*
https://www.adventure-journal.com/2017/03/what-everest-climber-really-meant-by-because-its-there/.

Unit 10: Emperor's Final New Year's Speech
"Republicanism in the United Kingdom".
https://en.wikipedia.org/wiki/Republicanism_in_the_United_Kingdom.

Unit 11: Better Investment with Gender Balance
Yuka Nakao. *"Feminist scholar calls Japan's gender problem 'human disaster'".*
https://english.kyodonews.net/news/2019/06/5fbad0a24182-feature-feminist-scholar-calls-japans-gender-problem-human-disaster.html.

Unit 12: Taiwan's First Same-Sex Marriages
Michael K. Lavers. *"Irish prime minister raises LGBTI issues during papal visit".*
https://www.washingtonblade.com/2018/08/26/irish-prime-minister-raises-lgbti-issues-during-papal-visit/.

Unit 13: Alabama Gets Strict Abortion Law
"Roe v. Wade".
https://www.history.com/topics/womens-rights/roe-v-wade.
"Roe v. Wade".
https://en.wikipedia.org/wiki/Roe_v._Wade.

Unit 14: Queen Elizabeth Gives Up Real Fur
"The ethics of speciesism".
http://www.bbc.co.uk/ethics/animals/rights/speciesism.shtml.

CNN ワールドニュース：文化・社会編

| 検印省略 | © 2021 年 1 月 31 日　初 版 発 行 |

編著者　　　　　　　　　真　野　　泰

発行者　　　　　　　　　原　　雅　久

発行所　　　　　　株式会社　朝 日 出 版 社

101-0065　東京都千代田区西神田 3-3-5
電話　東京　03-3239-0271
FAX　東京　03-3239-0479
e-mail　text-e@asahipress.com
振替口座　00140-2-46008
組版／イーズ　製版／錦明印刷

ISBN978-4-255-15669-9